# BLACK OR WHITE

## THAT'S ALRIGHT!

WRITTEN BY

TANYA P. MCLEAN - LOGAN

ISBN: 978-1-7773405-3-7 (Paperback)
ISBN: 978-1-7771506-6-2 (Hardcover)
ISBN:  978-1-7771506-4-8 (Electronic)

Any references to historical events, real people, or real places are used fictitiously. Names, characters, and places are products of the author's imagination.

Book formatting and illustrations by Disneyart

Printed by Amazon.ca, Ontario, Canada
First paperback edition December 2021
Second paperback edition January 2024

Published by: Arise Publications
Ajax, Ontario, Canada
Email: arisepublications1@gmail.com

This book is dedicated to every child (or adult)
who has faced some type of discrimination.
Always remember that you are special and unique.
Stay focused and committed in fulfilling
your goals and dreams in life.

Chanecia and Le-Sonn, I love you both to pieces.
You make my smile brighter every day.

NORA LIVES WITH HER MOM, DAD AND HER BROTHER JT IN A BIG CITY. HER DAD WORKS AS A BANKER WHILE HER MOM STAYS HOME TO TAKE CARE OF NORA AND JT.

NORA AND JT GO TO A SCHOOL THAT HAS A LOT OF PEOPLE FROM ALL OVER THE WORLD. IN THE SUMMERTIME, NORA AND JT ALWAYS ENJOY PLAYING WITH THE KIDS IN THE NEIGHBOURHOOD.

211

WELCOME!

T. McLean

THEY ESPECIALLY ENJOY PLAYING NAME THAT COUNTRY. BUT SOMETIMES THE KIDS WOULD GET MEAN AND CALL NORA A ZEBRA BECAUSE THEY WOULD SAY THAT SHE IS BLACK AND WHITE.

ONE DAY NORA CAME HOME FROM SCHOOL WHILE HER MOM WAS COOKING HER FAVOURITE DISH, LASAGNA. SHE CURIOUSLY ASKED, "MOM...WHY IS IT THAT YOU ARE WHITE, AND DAD IS BLACK?" NORA'S MOM PLACED THE LASAGNA IN THE OVEN, PUT THE OVEN MITTS ON TOP OF THE COUNTER AND HELD NORA'S HANDS.

MOM LOOKED IN HER EYES AND SMILED. SHE THEN SAID, "OH SUGAR, I KNEW YOU WOULD ASK THAT QUESTION SOMEDAY." NORA SMILED BACK AT HER MOTHER WITH A QUESTIONING LOOK ON HER FACE.

LIVE
LOVE
LAUGH

THEY BOTH WALKED OVER AND SAT DOWN AT THE KITCHEN TABLE. MOM BEGAN TELLING NORA WHY SHE HAD A WHITE MOM AND A BLACK DAD. HER MOM SAID, "WHEN YOUR DAD AND I MET, WE LIKED EACH OTHER AND THEN WE STARTED TO LOVE EACH OTHER." "A COUPLE OF YEARS WENT BY AND WE MET EACH OTHER'S FAMILY. WE WERE LIKE ONE BIG, HAPPY FAMILY.

WE THEN DECIDED TO GET MARRIED AND HAVE YOU AND JT." NORA SMILED, AND HER EYES TWINKLED WITH PLEASURE.

LIVE
LOVE
LAUGH

NORA'S MOM WENT ON TO TELL HER, "BABY GIRL WE ARE ALL EQUAL, BLACK OR WHITE...AND THAT'S ALRIGHT! IF YOU MEET SOMEONE THAT YOU LIKE, THEIR RACE OR SKIN COLOUR IS NOT SUPPOSED TO STOP YOU FROM BEING FRIENDS WITH THEM.

WE MAY LOOK DIFFERENT, BUT WE ARE ALL SPECIAL IN OUR OWN UNIQUE WAY."

NORA SMILED, AND HER FACE LIT UP WITH EXCITEMENT BECAUSE OF HER MOM'S STORY. NORA REALLY LIKED THE SOUND OF BEING FRIENDS WITH ANYONE NO MATTER WHAT THEIR RACE OR SKIN COLOUR MAY BE.

SHE THOUGHT EVERYONE SHOULD BE FRIENDS NO MATTER WHERE THEY'RE FROM. AFTER ALL, HER DADDY ALWAYS TOLD HER AND JT THAT THE WORLD IS ONE BIG FAMILY WITH PEOPLE SCATTERED ACROSS DIFFERENT PLACES.

WHEN DAD CAME HOME FROM WORK, NORA SAID, "DAD CAN I ASK YOU A QUESTION?" HER DAD HAD A PUZZLED LOOK ON HIS FACE. "WHAT NOW SWEET PEA?"

"WELL...WELL", NORA CONTINUED. "WHY IS IT THAT MOM IS WHITE, AND YOU ARE BLACK?"

NORA'S DAD SHOOK HIS HEAD, SIGHED AND SAID, "HONEY, BECAUSE WE LOVE EACH OTHER, YOUR MOM AND I SEE TWO BEAUTIFUL COLOURS, BLACK AND WHITE. WE SEE LOVE. WE LOVE EACH OTHER AND WE LOVE YOU AND JT."

HE WENT ON TO TELL NORA, "HONEY, WE ARE SUPPOSED TO LOVE AND RESPECT EVERYONE NO MATTER WHAT THEIR COLOUR IS, WHETHER RED, BLUE, GREEN, OR PURPLE." THEY BOTH GIGGLED TOGETHER. DAD CONTINUED, "SWEETHEART, IT SHOULDN'T MATTER WHERE SOMEONE IS FROM, WHAT THEIR RELIGION IS, OR EVEN IF THEY SPEAK DIFFERENTLY FROM YOU.

IT IS WRONG NOT TO LIKE SOMEONE BECAUSE THEY DON'T LOOK LIKE YOU OR HAVE THE SAME BACKGROUND AS YOU OR SOUND LIKE YOU. REMEMBER WHAT I ALWAYS TELL YOU AND JT, THAT THE WORLD IS ONE BIG FAMILY SCATTERED ACROSS DIFFERENT PLACES."

"YOUR MOTHER AND I HAVE THIS MOTTO AND WE STICK TO IT NO MATTER WHAT.

WE ALWAYS SAY BLACK OR WHITE, THAT'S ALRIGHT.

SEE BABY, FAMILIES ARE SUPPOSED TO LOVE EACH OTHER, BE KIND TO EACH OTHER AND TAKE CARE OF EACH OTHER. THE WORLD IS ONE BIG FAMILY AND WE ARE SUPPOSED TO LIVE IN LOVE, PEACE AND UNITY. WE SHOULD BE KIND TO EACH OTHER AND BE THERE FOR ONE ANOTHER. IF EVERYONE IN THE WORLD WOULD THINK LIKE THAT, WE WOULD HAVE MORE UNITY, LOVE AND RESPECT. REMEMBER THIS NORA, BLACK OR WHITE...THAT'S ALRIGHT!

NORA WAS SO EXCITED TO HEAR THOSE COMFORTING WORDS COMING FROM HER DAD'S MOUTH. SHE HUGGED HER DAD AND SAID, "DAD I LOVE YOU AND YOU ARE ALRIGHT. YOU ARE THE BEST DAD EVER!" DAD HAD THE BIGGEST AND PROUDEST SMILE ON HIS FACE.

NORA RAN OUTSIDE WITH A BURST OF EXCITEMENT. SHE COULDN'T WAIT TO SHARE WITH JT AND FRIENDS WHO WERE PLAYING MARBLES. NORA SHOUTED, "GUYS BLACK OR WHITE...THAT'S ALRIGHT!

SOME OF THE KIDS KNEW HOW HURT NORA WAS WHEN THEY CALLED HER NAMES, SO THEY WERE VERY SUPPORTIVE AND ACCEPTING OF HER. THE KIDS SMILED AND SAID WITH PLEASURE, "YEAH... BLACK OR WHITE...THAT'S ALRIGHT!

NORA THEN RAN TO HER NEIGHBOUR MRS. FERGUSON, AN OLD LADY WHO WOULD OFTEN COMFORT HER AS SHE CRIED WALKING HOME FROM SCHOOL AFTER BEING TEASED. MRS. FERGUSON WAS BUSY TENDING TO HER BEAUTIFUL FLOWER GARDEN. NORA SAID, "MRS. FERGUSON! MRS. FERGUSON! MY DAD SAID, BLACK OR WHITE, THAT'S ALRIGHT!

MRS. FERGUSON RAISED HER HEAD TO LOOK AT NORA WITH A WELCOMING SMILE ON HER FACE. WITH A CHEERFUL LOOK ON HER FACE SHE SAID, "YES MY DEAR CHILD, I'M GLAD YOU'VE FOUND IT OUT. GO SPREAD THE MESSAGE ACROSS THE WORLD!".

NORA'S FACE LIT UP LIKE THE SUN PIERCING THROUGH THE MIDDAY CLOUDS. SHE TOLD EVERYONE THAT SHE SAW ON THE STREET WHAT HER DAD HAD TOLD HER, "BLACK OR WHITE...THAT'S ALRIGHT!" BY THIS TIME, NORA HAD BECOME TIRED AND DECIDED TO HEAD BACK HOME TO HAVE DINNER WITH HER FAMILY.

ALL THE WAY HOME, HER SMILE RADIATED THROUGH THE NEIGHBOURHOOD. EVERYONE WAS HAPPY THAT THIS LITTLE GIRL HAD BROUGHT SO MUCH JOY WITH HER PARENT'S SLOGAN, "BLACK OR WHITE...THAT'S ALRIGHT!" THEY ALL CHEERED HER ON AS SHE WALKED BY AND CHANTED THE NEW MOTTO, "BLACK OR WHITE...THAT'S ALRIGHT!"

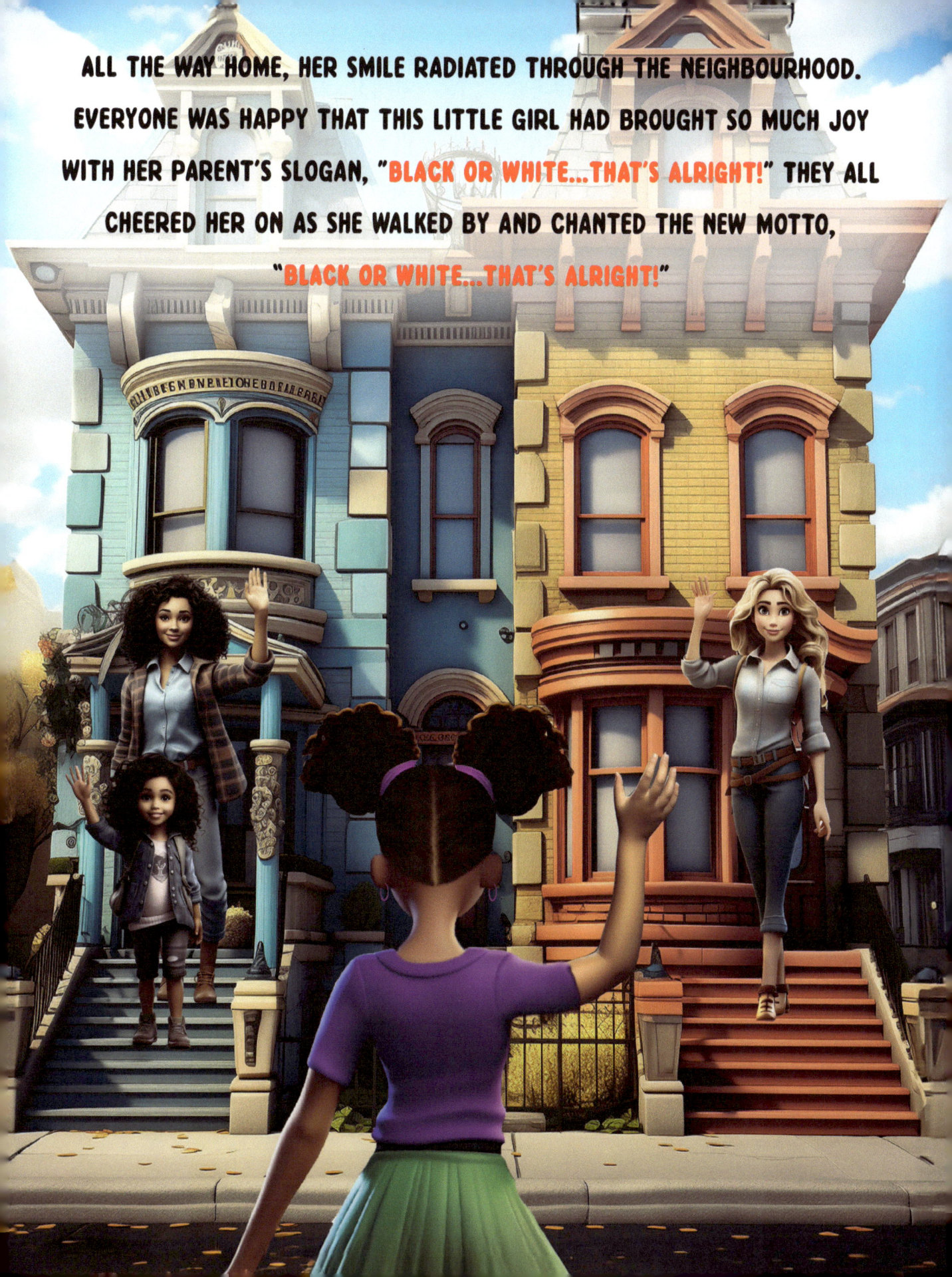

EVERYONE STARTED HUGGING EACH OTHER BECAUSE THEY FELT A FLOW OF LOVE, PEACE, JOY, STRENGTH AND ACCEPTANCE AMONGEST EVERYONE IN THE COMMUNITY. THEY WERE LIKE BROTHERS AND SISTERS LIVING IN HARMONY. THIS WAS FROM THE ABUNDANCE OF LOVE THAT ONE LITTLE GIRL BROUGHT TO THEIR COMMUNITY.

NORA'S PARENTS HEARD THE UPROAR COMING DOWN THE STREET. THEY WENT OUTSIDE TO SEE WHAT WAS HAPPENING. EVERYONE WAS SHOUTING, "BLACK OR WHITE...THAT'S ALRIGHT!" IMMEDIATELY, THEY LOOKED AT EACH OTHER AND SMILED BECAUSE THEY KNEW IT WAS NORA'S DOING.

THEY SET OUT TO MEET HER AND GAVE HER A BIG WELCOME HOME HUG. JT, WHO WAS STILL PLAYING MARBLES WITH HIS FRIENDS, TOLD THEM GOODBYE AND JOINED HIS FAMILY. THEY FELT GOOD AND WERE PLEASED WITH THE UNITY NORA HAD BROUGHT TO THE COMMUNITY.

IT WAS NOW GETTING LATE, SO THEY WAVED GOODBYE TO THEIR FRIENDS AND WENT INSIDE THE HOUSE.

THE FOUR HUGGED EACH OTHER AND SAID, "BLACK OR WHITE...THAT'S ALRIGHT!" THEN JT SAID, "WE'RE ALRIGHT!" MOM SENT THE KIDS TO WASH THEIR HANDS FOR DINNER.

THEY THEN SAT DOWN AT THE TABLE TO EAT MOM'S DELICIOUS LASAGNA AND SPINACH SALAD.

NORA WENT TO THE FRIDGE TO GET HER FAVOURITE DRINK, ICED-COLD, COCONUT WATER.

NORA HAD NO IDEA WHAT SHE HAD DONE IN THE COMMUNITY. THE NEXT DAY ALL THE NEIGHBOURS WERE TALKING ABOUT NORA AND HER DETERMINATION TO MAKE SURE PEOPLE TREAT EACH OTHER WITH RESPECT, KINDNESS AND CARE.

AS NORA TOOK THE BUS TO SCHOOL THAT MORNING, SHE SAID GOOD MORNING TO MR. SIMMS THE BUS DRIVER. SHE TOLD HIM ABOUT WHAT HAD HAPPENED THE NIGHT BEFORE. MR. SIMMS WAS HAPPY ABOUT WHAT NORA HAD DONE. HE TOLD HER THAT HE HAD AN IDEA.

HE FELT SYMPATHY FOR HER BECAUSE SHE WAS OFTEN SAD AT THE END OF EACH SCHOOL DAY.

THAT DAY AFTER SCHOOL, THE CHILDREN WERE ALL LINED UP TO CATCH THE SCHOOL BUS TO GO HOME. TO THEIR AMAZEMENT, MR. SIMMS HAD A BIG BANNER INSIDE THE WINDSHIELD OF THE BUS. EVERYONE GOT CLOSER TO SEE WHAT IT SAID AS THE BUS PULLED IN.

THE BANNER READ, "BLACK OR WHITE...THAT'S ALRIGHT!" WITH ZEBRA STRIPES DECORATED AROUND IT. NORA SAID, "GUYS LOOK! LOOK WHAT MR. SIMMS HAS DONE."

SCHOOL BUS

BLACK OR WHITE THAT'S ALRIGHT !

ABCD

NORA GOT ON FIRST AND GAVE HIM A BIG HUG. WITH TEARS IN HER EYES, SHE SAID, "THANK YOU, MR. SIMMS, THANK YOU!" MR. SIMMS SAID, "YOU'RE WELCOME NORA. THAT'S THE LEAST I COULD DO TO HELP SPREAD YOUR MESSAGE OF LOVE." "BLACK OR WHITE...THAT'S ALRIGHT!"

MR. SIMMS THEN TOOK UP THE BANNER AND TAPED IT IN A SAFE SPOT, ACROSS THE TOP WHERE ALL THE STUDENTS COULD READ IT. THE CHILDREN WENT HOME CHANTING "BLACK OR WHITE...THAT'S ALRIGHT! BLACK OR WHITE...IT'S ALRIGHT!".

USUALLY, MR. SIMMS WOULDN'T ALLOW THAT MUCH NOISE ON THE BUS, BUT THIS TIME, HE DIDN'T MIND. THE CHILDREN WERE HAPPY AND SO WAS HE.

# WORDS AND DEFINITIONS

Neighbourhood - the people living near one another

Race - a group of people sharing a common culture, language, religion or background

Unique - being the only one

Puzzled - confused because you do not understand something

Unity - joined together or in agreement

Harmony - people living or working happily together without any big problems

Determination – continuing to do something even if it is hard

Sympathy - caring for someone else who is suffering or has problems that made them unhappy

Radiated - to send out heat or light

Acceptance - agreeing to something

Abundance - an amount that is more than enough

Amazement - to cause someone to be very surprised

# Canadian Web-Based Diversity Resources

Affiliation of Multicultural Societies and Service Agencies (AMSSA) of BC offers a centralized resource for the settlement and immigration sector, regarding issues involving multiculturalism, immigration and human rights.

Amnesty International Canada has a youth section that offers excellent support and resources on taking action on rights issues around the world.

Anima Leadership offers innovative professional training centred around diversity and social justice issues that dares individuals to explore and develop their leadership potential.

Black North Initiative is an initiative created by The Canadian Council of Business Leaders Against Anti-Black Systemic to increase the representation of Blacks in boardrooms and executive suites across Canada.

Black Youth Helpline serves all youth and specifically responds to the need for a Black youth specific service, positioned and resourced to promote access to professional, culturally appropriate support for youth, families and schools.

British Columbia Teachers' Federation (BCTF) has an ambitious Social Justice Program and their web site features a range of events, programs, links, lesson aids, resources, funding opportunities and more.

Canadian Anti-racism Education and Research Society has a website with useful links and ideas. CAER is a front-line, grassroots anti-racist organization that tracks, monitors and fights racism and hate crime, lobbies governments and agencies to provide support for human rights, and supports other organizations and agencies that provide human rights education and research world-wide.

Canadian Centre for Diversity and Inclusion is a made-in-Canada solution designed to help employers, diversity and inclusion/ human rights/equity, and human resources practitioners effectively address the full picture of diversity, equity and inclusion within the workplace.

Canadian Council for Refugees is a non-profit umbrella organization committed to the rights and protection of refugees in Canada and around the world and to the settlement of refugees and immigrants in Canada.

Canadian Diversity is a journal produced by the Association for Canadian Studies, which also has links and research information for students, professors and researchers with an interest in diversity issues.

Canadian Ethnic Studies Association is a non-profit interdisciplinary organization devoted to the study of ethnicity, multiculturalism, immigration, inter-group relations and the cultural life of ethnic groups in Canada, and publishes a regular e-bulletin, a scholarly journal, and has other resources.

Canadian Immigrant Magazine is a free monthly magazine, a vibrant and informative source of stories, resources, business and community links related to immigration and settlement in Canada. It features pieces on careers, housing, health, education and culture, among other topics.

Canadian Race Relations Foundation is Canada's leading agency dedicated to the elimination of racism in the country. They host a national conference and awards program, and their website offers news, educational resources, funding programs and numerous publications on racism-related issues.

Canadian Red Cross has various educational and youth programs aimed at preventing and eliminating violence, bullying, and abuse.

Canadian Teachers' Federation has a number of programs and resources related to diversity, social justice, Aboriginal education and anti-discrimination.

Centre for Culture, Identity and Education (CCIE) was established at UBC in 2005 and explores cultural studies and identity toward the promotion of local, national and global cultural and activist work and research.

Centre for Social Justice conducts research, education and advocacy to enhance peace and security, to narrow gaps in income, wealth and power, and to promote greater equality and democracy. They are based in Montreal and have a number of good publications and events.

Check Your Head is a youth-driven organization that provides education for young people on issues such as democracy, corporate power, globalization and climate change to encourage informed, empowered and active young people.

Choose Your Voice is a free resource designed as part of the "Fighting Anti-Semitism Together" (FAST) project. It helps students learn about the dangers of hatred and stereotypes and find their voices to combat them. It encourages students not to be bystanders or perpetrators, but heroes, by speaking out.

Classroom Connections is Canadian non-profit organization that develops free educational resources for schools, addressing areas that may not typically be covered in classroom text books, such as global citizenship, economic disparity, fair trade, sustainable development and peace education.

Diversity Institute at Ryerson University has a useful resource list of grassroots, advocacy and affiliate groups promoting cultural or diversity issues.

Federation of Black Canadians is a national, non-profit organization, driven by organizations across the country that advances the social, economic, political and cultural interests of Canadians of African descent.

Harmony Movement is a not-for-profit organization to combat racism and discrimination and promotes youth leadership through education.

How Indigenous Knowledge Advances Modern Science and Technology takes a look throughout history, Indigenous peoples have been responsible for the development of many technologies and have substantially contributed to science.

Human Rights Research and Education Centre is run by the University of Ottawa. Since May 1981, they have been exploring linkages between human rights, governance, legal reform and development, supporting national human rights institutions in Canada and abroad, and engaging in multidisciplinary research and education.

Interfaith Unity Newsletter is a free newsletter of Interfaith activities, news and resources in Toronto, Southern Ontario and internationally.

League for Human Rights of B'Nai Brith Canada has produced a number of educational programs and resources on anti-hate activity.

Learning the Land program combines Indigenous teachings with scientific knowledge. Learning the Land is a program created by the Nature Conservancy of Canada and the Treaty 4 Education Alliance. It combines Indigenous culture and teachings with scientific knowledge about conservation.

London Cross Cultural Learner Centre has been open for over 50 years and offers excellent listing of diversity resources and services.

Media Smarts has a number of excellent resources for teachers and parents related to digital media and information literacy, on the themes of cultural diversity, racism, representation, and bias.

Me to We is a for-profit venture offering products and services related to finding meaning in our lives and world by reaching out to others. Marc and Craig Kiel-burger, founders of Free The Children, have worked in numerous countries with some spiritual, political and social leaders of our time.

Multiculturalism through the Government of Canada celebrates and preserves the history and heritage of Canada's various ethnic groups and contains information on relevant resources and events.

Not in Our Town is a hate crime prevention initiative based in Surrey, BC. This project aims to involve residents in exploring issues related to hate activity (racism, sexism, homophobia, or any other form of discrimination that victimizes their community), to discuss their hopes, and develop action plans for the community.

Ontario Black History Society is a non-profit registered Canadian charity dedicated to the study, preservation and promotion of Black History and heritage. The OBHS fosters the recognition, preservation and promotion of the contributions of Black peoples and their collective histories through education, research and cooperation, sponsoring educational conferences and exhibits, and including material on Black History in school curricula.

Ontario Human Rights Commission has a number of good resources and guides around human rights and discrimination issues. Safe Harbour: Respect for All is a four-province initiative to assist businesses, institutions, agencies and entire municipalities to celebrate differences and create safer, more welcoming communities that reject discrimination.

Statistics Canada has a wealth of information on Canadian ethnic diversity and immigration, including detailed results from the 2002 Ethnic Diversity Survey.

Stop Racism and Hate Collective is a group that monitors hate group activity, helps young people leave hate groups, and provides information and advice to help stop hate motivated activity on the Internet and in communities.

Students Helping Others Understand Tolerance (SHOUT) is a national organization, founded and governed by students. They promote genocide awareness and speaking out against racism and intolerance both across Canada and within the global sphere.

The Black Liberation Collective is an international movement of students challenging anti-Black racism in post-secondary institutions in every way that it manifests.

The Canadian Human Rights Commission (CHRC) was established in 1977 by the government of Canada. It is empowered under the Canadian Human Rights Act to investigate and try to settle complaints of discrimination in employment and in the provision of services within federal jurisdiction.

Youth Action Network is a national non-profit youth organization dedicated to helping youth become more informed and actively involved in order to move towards a just and sustainable society.

United Nations Association in Canada has a Canada's Diversity Advantage program that offers a multi-generational and multicultural initiative of Canadians' lived-experiences, to cultivate a deeper understanding of how diverse cultures, faiths and ideas have contributed to building a diverse and inclusive society shaped by many cultures.

University of Victoria's Equity and Human Rights Office has a section within their website with resources for building an inclusive community.

Vancouver Holocaust Education Centre (VHEC) is a non-profit society that combats prejudice, racism and anti-Semitism by educating the public, especially students and teachers, about the events and implications of the Holocaust. The VHEC mounts traveling educational exhibits, organizes scholarly and educational conferences, and produces and circulates outreach discovery kits, curriculum materials, Teachers Guides and online interactive media.

# About the Author

**Tanya P. McLean - Logan**

Tanya McLean – Logan has been an educator in Ontario, Canada for over twenty years. She completed her Bachelor of Professional Studies degree in teacher education from Niagara University. She has a bachelor's degree in Early Childhood Education from Toronto Metropolitan University, formerly known as Ryerson University and a Master of Divinity degree from Canada Christian College. She is a wife and mother of two wonderful children. Her passion is writing and working in the field of special education, equity and diversity.

As a young child, Tanya has always had a love for everyone. She often reached out to people that others overlooked or made fun of, like the mentally ill. The young schoolgirl, Tanya, saw mentally ill people walking on the street, sitting in pity, eating from the garbage and being mistreated and shunned by others in Jamaica. Tanya's tender heart always wanted to reach out to them, and one day, she did. Tanya's compassion allowed her to use her lunch money to buy food for mentally ill people because she didn't think they deserved to go hungry. She often sat and chatted with them, while her friends ran away and thought she was crazy for doing so.

As an adult, Tanya has not changed. Being an educator, she has seen children being made fun of for many reasons. It hurts her to see anyone treated unfairly because of the colour of their skin, their mental state, their religion, their race, gender or any other orientation. Everyone is unique and special in their own way. Therefore, everyone should treat others just the way they want to be treated. If we all start doing this, the world would be a better place.

# About the Illustrator

**Disneyart**

Disney completed her Specialist Honors graphic designing at the University of LUMS. She has a designing advanced diploma from Superior College and a B.Ed. from University of LUMS. Disney is a freelance artist in Punjab.